United States Government Accountability Office

Report to Congressional Committees

I0455239

May 2013

DEFENSE ACQUISITIONS

Continued Management Attention Needed to Enhance Use and Review of DOD's Inventory of Contracted Services

GAO-13-491

GAO Highlights

Highlights of GAO-13-491, a report to congressional committees

DEFENSE ACQUISITIONS

Continued Management Attention Needed to Enhance Use and Review of DOD's Inventory of Contracted Services

Why GAO Did This Study

DOD is the government's largest purchaser of contractor-provided services. In fiscal year 2011, DOD reported $199 billion in obligations for service contracts, which include services as varied as medical services and intelligence support. In 2008, Congress required DOD to compile and review an annual inventory of its contracted services to include the number of contractors providing services to DOD and the functions these contractors were performing. The 2010 National Defense Authorization Act directed GAO to report for 3 years on these inventories.

For this third report, GAO assessed (1) the progress DOD has made in compiling the fiscal year 2011 inventory of contracted services and efforts to collect contractor manpower data, and (2) the extent to which defense components complied with DOD's guidance for reporting on their inventory reviews. GAO reviewed relevant laws and guidance, analyzed inventory submissions from 31 components, reviewed component certification letters, and interviewed DOD acquisition and manpower officials.

What GAO Recommends

GAO recommends that the Secretary of Defense direct component heads to discuss in their certification letters all required inventory review elements, as well as how instances where contractors are performing inherently governmental functions were resolved. DOD generally concurred with our recommendations, but indicated that the Secretary's involvement was not necessary. GAO believes it is, as discussed in the report.

View GAO-13-491. For more information, contact Timothy J. DiNapoli at (202) 512-4841 or dinapolit@gao.gov.

What GAO Found

Over the past year and a half, the Department of Defense (DOD) has taken steps to implement its plan to collect contractor manpower data directly from contractors and to develop and implement a department-wide system, based on the Army's existing system, to collect and store these and other inventory data. DOD officials estimate that the data system will be available in fiscal year 2014, with DOD components reporting on most of their service contracts by fiscal year 2016. DOD, however, is still working on key decisions related to security, funding, and other technological issues and has not developed a plan of action with anticipated time frames and necessary resources to help ensure DOD remains on track to meet its goals. Making timely decisions and developing a plan of action with anticipated timeframes and necessary resources, as GAO has previously recommended, would facilitate DOD's stated intent of implementing a DOD-wide system to collect required inventory information. For the fiscal year 2011 inventory, DOD components generally used the same compilation processes used in the previous year. As such, with the exception of the Army, which already has an inventory data collection system, the remaining components relied primarily on the Federal Procurement Data System-Next Generation (FPDS-NG). GAO previously reported that FPDS-NG has several limitations, including the inability to identify more than one type of service in a contract or the number of contractor full-time equivalents (FTE), which limit its utility for purposes of compiling a complete and accurate inventory.

Consistent with DOD's December 2011 guidance, 29 of the 31 components submitted letters certifying that they had conducted an inventory review as of April 2013. DOD officials stated that the requirement to submit certification letters represented a significant improvement over prior years' reviews, when DOD could not determine whether the required reviews were conducted. These officials also stated that the letters provided useful insights into the components' efforts. GAO's analysis, however, indicates that none of the components' certification letters discussed all six elements required by DOD's guidance. For example, GAO's analysis found that the letters generally provided only limited information on their review methodologies or the results of their review efforts. In addition, it is unclear based on the information provided in the certification letters the extent to which the differences in the methodologies components used to conduct the reviews contributed to the variation in the identification of contractors performing inherently governmental functions, unauthorized personal services, or closely associated with inherently governmental functions. For example, the Army, using its review process, identified over 44,000 contractor FTEs performing closely associated with inherently governmental functions, while the Air Force identified about 1,400 contractor FTEs and 13 components reported they had no contractors performing these functions. Further, the Army and the Air Force did not provide complete information on actions taken to resolve instances where they had identified contractors performing inherently governmental functions as part of their reviews, such as by transferring performance of these functions to DOD personnel or modifying the contract's statement of work. The ability to identify contractors performing these functions is valuable as it allows actions to be taken, but that value is significantly reduced if decision-makers have no assurance as to whether corrective actions were taken.

Contents

Abbreviations

AT&L	Office of the Under Secretary of Defense for Acquisition, Technology and Logistics
CMRA	Contractor Manpower Reporting Application
DLA	Defense Logistics Agency
DISA	Defense Information Systems Agency
DOD	Department of Defense
eCMRA	Enterprise-wide Contractor Manpower Reporting Application
FPDS-NG	Federal Procurement Data System-Next Generation
FTE	full-time equivalent
P&R	Office of the Under Secretary of Defense for Personnel and Readiness

GAO U.S. GOVERNMENT ACCOUNTABILITY OFFICE

441 G St. N.W.
Washington, DC 20548

May 23, 2013

The Honorable Carl Levin
Chairman
The Honorable James M. Inhofe
Ranking Member
Committee on Armed Services
United States Senate

The Honorable Howard P. "Buck" McKeon
Chairman
The Honorable Adam Smith
Ranking Member
Committee on Armed Services
House of Representatives

The Department of Defense (DOD) is the federal government's largest purchaser of contractor-provided services, reporting about $199 billion in obligations for contracted services in fiscal year 2011. DOD relies on contractors to perform various functions, such as professional and management support, medical services, information technology support, and weapon system and intelligence support. While there are benefits to using contractors to perform services for the government, our prior work has shown that reliance on contractors to support core missions can place the government at risk of becoming overly reliant on contractors to perform closely associated with inherently governmental functions or creating circumstances in which contractors perform functions deemed inherently governmental.[1] Over the past decade, our work has also identified the need for DOD to obtain better data on its contracted services to enable it to make more strategic decisions.[2] While DOD has begun a number of efforts to gain better insight into its acquisition of services, these efforts have had mixed success to date.

In recent years, Congress has enacted legislation to improve DOD's ability to manage its acquisition of services; to make more strategic decisions about the right workforce mix of military, civilian, and contractor personnel; and to better align resource needs through the budget process to achieve that mix. For example, Section 2330a of title 10 of the U.S. Code requires DOD to annually compile and review an inventory of activities performed by contractors pursuant to contracts for services to, among other things, help provide better insight into the number of contractor full-time equivalents (FTE) providing services to the department and the functions they are performing and determine whether any of these functions warrant conversion to DOD civilian performance.[3]

---

[1]GAO, *Defense Management: DOD Needs to Reexamine Its Extensive Reliance on Contractors and Continue to Improve Management and Oversight,* GAO-08-572T (Washington, D.C.: Mar. 11, 2008). Inherently governmental functions are defined by law as functions that are so intimately related to the public interest as to require performance by federal government employees. Federal Activities Inventory Reform (FAIR) Act of 1998, Pub. L. No 105-270, § 5; 31 U.S.C. § 501, note. There is currently an open Federal Acquisition Regulation (FAR) case (2012-001) under consideration to implement a September 2011 Office of Federal Procurement Policy Letter that, among other things, clarified the definition of "inherently governmental function" (consistent with the FAIR Act definition). Office of Federal Procurement Policy, Policy Letter 11-01, *Performance of Inherently Governmental and Critical Functions* (Sept. 12, 2011). In addition, closely associated with inherently governmental functions are those that while not inherently governmental, may approach the category because of the nature of the function, the manner in which the contractor performs the contract, or the manner in which the government administers performance under a contract. FAR § 7.503(d) provides examples of such functions.

[2]See, for example, GAO, *Strategic Sourcing: Improved and Expanded Use Could Save Billions in Annual Procurement Costs,* GAO-12-919 (Washington, D.C.: Sept. 20, 2012); *Defense Acquisitions: Actions Needed to Ensure Value for Service Contracts,* GAO-09-643T (Washington, D.C.: Apr. 23, 2009); and *Defense Acquisitions: Tailored Approach Needed to Improve Service Acquisition Outcomes,* GAO-07-20 (Washington, D.C.: Nov. 9, 2006).

[3]An FTE is a standard measure of labor that equates to one year of full-time work (labor hours as defined by the Office of Management and Budget Circular A-11 each year). To report the number of contractor FTEs, one would divide the number of direct labor hours reported by a contractor for each service by 2,088, the number of labor hours in a federal employee work year.

DOD has submitted annual inventories for fiscal years 2007 through 2011, the most recent submitted on August 27, 2012.

Section 803(c) of the National Defense Authorization Act for fiscal year 2010 directed GAO to report for 3 years on the inventory of activities performed pursuant to contracts for services that are to be submitted by the Secretary of Defense for fiscal years 2009, 2010, and 2011 respectively.[4] To respond to this mandate, we first issued a report in January 2011 that assessed the approaches used to compile the fiscal year 2009 inventories.[5] In that report, we recommended that DOD develop a plan of action to facilitate the department's stated intent of collecting contractor manpower data directly from contractors and to address other limitations in its approach to meeting the statutory inventory requirements, including those specific to the Federal Procurement Data System-Next Generation (FPDS-NG). This system has a number of limitations, including that it does not identify more than one type of service purchased for each contract action.

We issued a second report in April 2012 that assessed the progress DOD had made in addressing limitations in compiling the fiscal year 2010 inventory, and the extent to which the military departments addressed issues with contractors performing inherently governmental functions identified during their reviews of the fiscal year 2009 inventories.[6] We found that DOD, with the exception of the Army, had much further to go in addressing the requirements for compiling and reviewing the inventories of contracted services. For example, we reported that the Navy had no assurance that their commands conducted the required reviews and found no evidence that the required reviews were conducted at the Navy commands we contacted. In addition, we found that in certain cases, contractors continued to perform functions the military departments identified as inherently governmental. We recommended that the Secretary of Defense ensure that the military departments and defense components issue guidance to their commands to provide for clear lines

---

[4]Pub. L. No. 111-84 (2009).

[5]GAO, *Defense Acquisitions: Further Action Needed to Better Implement Requirements for Conducting Inventory of Service Contract Activities*, GAO-11-192 (Washington, D.C.: Jan. 14, 2011).

[6]GAO, *Defense Acquisitions: Further Actions Needed to Improve Accountability for DOD's Inventory of Contracted Services,* GAO-12-357 (Washington, D.C.: Apr. 6, 2012).

GAO-13-491 DOD Inventory of Contracted Services

of authority, responsibility, and accountability for conducting an inventory review and resolving instances where functions being performed by contractors are identified as inherently governmental functions. DOD agreed it was imperative for the components to do so, but noted that its December 2011 guidance regarding the submission and review of the fiscal year 2011 inventories, while not prescribing individual component management practices, requires component heads to certify completion of and results from the reviews.

This report is our third and final review in response to the mandate and focuses on DOD's fiscal year 2011 inventory. We assessed (1) the progress DOD has made in compiling the inventory of contracted services and the status of efforts to collect contractor manpower data and (2) the extent to which the defense components complied with DOD's December 2011 guidance for reporting on their reviews of the fiscal year 2011 inventories.

To conduct our work, we reviewed relevant guidance related to the inventory compilation and review processes and interviewed officials from the Office of the Under Secretary of Defense for Acquisition, Technology and Logistics (AT&L); Office of Defense Procurement and Acquisition Policy; the Office of the Under Secretary of Defense for Personnel and Readiness (P&R); the Office of the Under Secretary of Defense (Comptroller); the departments of the Army, Navy, Air Force; and two selected DOD components—the Defense Logistics Agency (DLA) and Defense Information Systems Agency (DISA)—based on the number of contractor FTEs they identified.

To assess the progress DOD has made in compiling the inventory of contracted services and the status of efforts to collect contractor manpower data, we analyzed 31 components' inventory submissions and all memorandums accompanying their inventory submissions to determine the methodologies used to compile their fiscal year 2011 inventory and to calculate or estimate the number of contractor FTEs and obtained information on the department's efforts to collect contractor manpower data. We include DOD's estimate of overall obligations and contractor FTEs for fiscal year 2011 in this report. We did not independently assess the accuracy or reliability of the underlying data supporting the components' inventories of contracted services. However, our previous work identified data limitations with DOD components using data from FPDS-NG as the basis for their inventories. We discuss these limitations in the report, as appropriate.

To assess the extent to which components complied with DOD's December 2011 guidance on the inventory review process, we reviewed all 29 fiscal year 2011 inventory review certification letters submitted by DOD components as of April 2013. We assessed the letters to determine if components reported on the six elements in DOD's guidance for the inventory review, including the selection criteria and methodologies used to conduct the reviews, the extent to which contractors were found to be performing certain functions, to include inherently governmental and closely associated with inherently governmental, and to the extent necessary, a plan to realign performance of such functions to government performance. A detailed description of our scope and methodology is included in appendix I.

We conducted this performance audit from October 2012 to May 2013 in accordance with generally accepted auditing standards. Those standards require that we plan and perform the audit to obtain sufficient, appropriate evidence to provide a reasonable basis for our findings and conclusions based on our audit objectives. We believe that the evidence obtained provides a reasonable basis for our findings and conclusions based on audit objectives.

Background

In part to improve the availability of information on and management of DOD's acquisition of services, in fiscal year 2002 Congress enacted section 2330a of title 10 of the U.S. Code, which required the Secretary of Defense to establish a data collection system to provide management information on each purchase of services by a military department or defense agency.[7] The information to be collected includes, among other things, the services purchased, the total dollar amount of the purchase, the form of contracting action used to make the purchase, and the extent of competition provided in making the purchase.

In 2008, Congress amended section 2330a to add a requirement for the Secretary of Defense to submit an annual inventory of the activities performed pursuant to contracts for services for or on behalf of DOD

---

[7]The National Defense Authorization Act for Fiscal Year 2002, Pub. L. No. 107-107, § 801(c) (2001).

during the preceding fiscal year.[8] The inventory is to include a number of specific data elements for each identified activity, including

- the function and missions performed by the contractor;
- the contracting organization, the component of DOD administering the contract, and the organization whose requirements are being met through contractor performance of the function;
- the funding source for the contract by appropriation and operating agency;
- the fiscal year the activity first appeared on an inventory;
- the number of contractor employees (expressed as FTEs) for direct labor, using direct labor hours and associated cost data collected from contractors;
- a determination of whether the contract pursuant to which the activity is performed is a personal services contract,[9] and
- a summary of the information required by section 2330a(a) of title 10 of the U.S. Code.

As implemented by DOD, components are to compile annual inventories of activities performed on their behalf by contractors and submit them to AT&L, which is to formally submit a consolidated DOD inventory to Congress no later than June 30. Since this provision was implemented DOD-wide, the primary source used by DOD components, with the exception of the Army, to compile their inventories has been FPDS-NG. The Army developed its Contractor Manpower Reporting Application (CMRA) in 2005 to collect information on labor-hour expenditures by function, funding source, and mission supported on contracted efforts, and has used CMRA as the basis for its inventory. CMRA captures data directly reported by contractors on services performed at the contract line item level, including information on the direct labor dollars, direct labor hours, total invoiced dollars, the functions and mission performed, and the organizational unit on whose behalf the services are being performed. In instances where contractors are providing different services under the

---

[8]The National Defense Authorization Act for Fiscal Year 2008, Pub. L. No. 110-181, § 807.

[9]A personal services contract is characterized by the employer-employee relationship it creates between the government and the contractor's personnel. The government is normally required to obtain its employees by direct hire under competitive appointment or other procedures required by the civil service laws. Agencies are not permitted to award personal services contracts unless specifically authorized by statute to do so. FAR § 37.104.

same order, or are providing services at multiple locations, contractors can enter additional records in CMRA to capture information associated with each type of service or location. It also allows for the identification of services provided under contracts for goods.

Within 30 days after it is submitted to Congress, the inventory is to be made public. Within 90 days of the date on which the inventory is submitted to Congress, the Secretaries of the military department and heads of the defense agencies responsible for activities in the inventory are to complete a review of the contracts and activities for which they are responsible and ensure that any personal services contracts in the inventory were properly entered into and performed appropriately; that the activities in the inventory do not include inherently governmental functions; that to the maximum extent practicable, the activities on the list do not include any functions closely associated with inherently governmental functions; and that activities that should be considered for conversion to DOD civilian performance have been identified.[10]

In January 2011, Congress amended section 2330a(c) of title 10 of the U.S. Code to specify that P&R, AT&L, and Comptroller are responsible for issuing guidance for compiling the inventory.[11] Section 2330a(c) was also amended to state that DOD is to use direct labor hours and associated cost data collected from contractors as the basis for the number of contactor FTEs identified in the inventory, though it provided that DOD may use estimates where such data are not available and cannot reasonably be made available in a timely manner.

Congress provided further direction on the collection of FTE information for contractor employees in the Department of Defense and Full-Year Continuing Appropriations Act, 2011 by providing not less than $2 million to both the Navy and Air Force to leverage the Army's CMRA to document the number of full-time contractor employees, or their equivalent in the inventory. The services and the directors of the defense agencies in coordination with P&R were to report to the Congressional defense committees within 60 days of enactment of that act on their plans

---

[10]10 U.S.C. § 2330a(e).

[11]The Ike Skelton National Defense Authorization Act for Fiscal Year 2011, Pub. L. No. 111-383, § 321.

GAO-13-491 DOD Inventory of Contracted Services

for documenting the number of full-time contractor employees or their equivalent.[12]

In December 2011, section 936 of the National Defense Authorization Act for Fiscal Year 2012 amended section 2330a of title 10 of the U.S. Code to clarify the types of contracted services to be inventoried, including contracts for goods to the extent services are a significant component of performance, as identified in a separate line item of a contract. This section also directed the secretary of the military department or head of the defense agency responsible for activities in the inventory to develop a plan, including an enforcement mechanism and approval process, to

- provide for the use of the inventory to make determinations regarding the most appropriate mix of military, civilian, and contractor personnel to perform its mission;
- ensure that the inventory is used to inform strategic workforce planning;
- facilitate the use of the inventory for budgetary purposes; and
- provide for appropriate consideration of the conversion of certain activities, to include those closely associated with inherently governmental functions, critical functions, and acquisition workforce functions, to performance by government employees.[13]

Section 2463 of title 10 of the U.S. Code requires the Secretary of Defense to make use of the inventory of contracted services to identify certain functions performed by contractors, to include closely associated with inherently governmental functions, critical functions and acquisition workforce functions, and ensure that special consideration is given to converting those functions to civilian performance.

Further, the National Defense Authorization Act for Fiscal Year 2010 provided for a new section 115b in title 10 of the U.S. Code that requires DOD to annually submit to the defense committees a strategic workforce plan to shape and improve the civilian workforce. Among other requirements, the plan is to include an assessment of the appropriate mix of military, civilian, and contractor personnel capabilities. P&R is responsible for developing and implementing the strategic plan in consultation with AT&L. The act also added section 235 to title 10 of the

---

[12]Pub. L. No. 112-10, § 8108.

[13] Pub.L.No.112-81.

U.S. Code, which requires that the Secretary of Defense include (in the budget justification materials submitted to Congress) information that clearly and separately identifies both the amount requested for the procurement of contract services for each DOD component, installation, or activity and the number of contractor employee full-time equivalents projected and justified for each DOD component, installation, or activity based on the inventory of contracts for services and associated reviews.[14]

Collectively, these statutory requirements mandate the use of the inventory and the associated review process to enhance the ability of DOD to identify and track the services provided by contractors, achieve accountability for the contractor sector of its total workforce, help identify functions for possible conversion from contractor performance to DOD civilian performance, support the development of DOD's annual strategic workforce plan, and project and justify the number of contractor FTEs included in its annual budget justification materials. Figure 1 illustrates the relationship among the related statutory requirements.

---

[14]Pub. L. No. 111-84 § 1108(a)(1) and 803 (a)(1) (2009).

Figure 1: Relationship among the Inventory of Contracted Services, Insourcing, and Budget Documentation Requirements

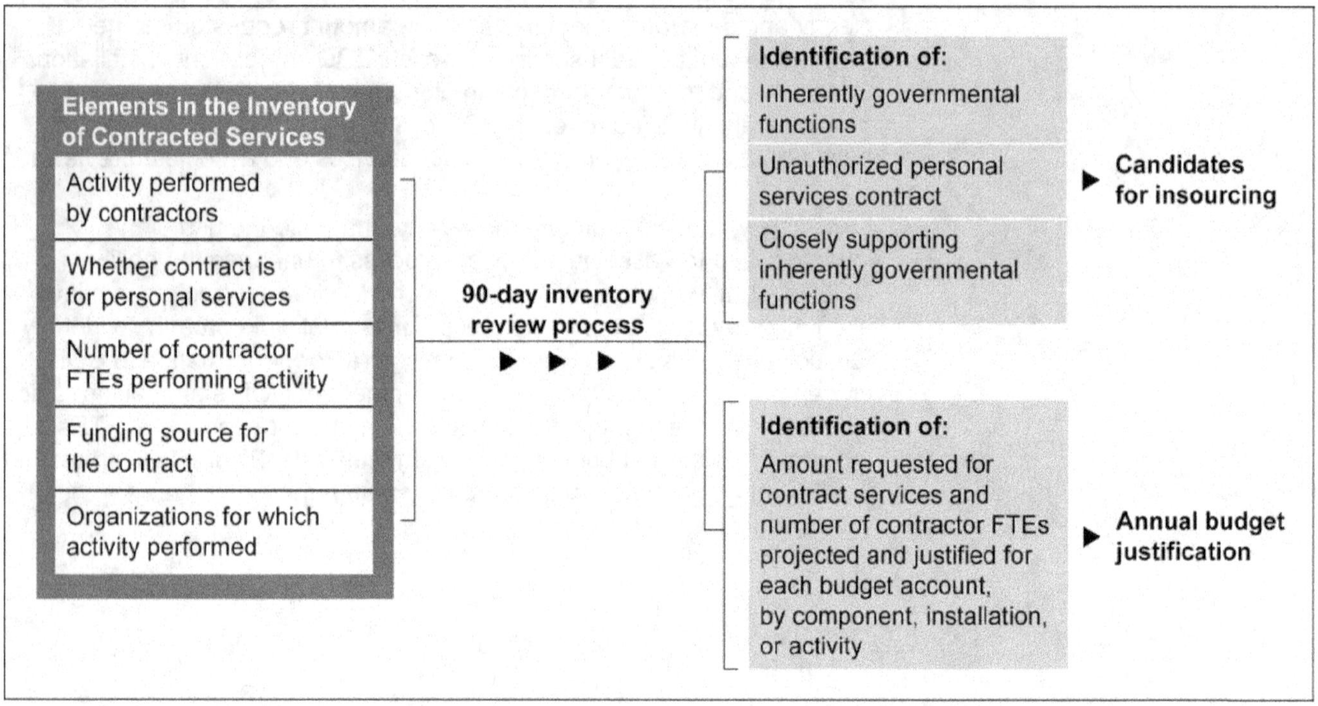

Source: GAO analysis of 10 U.S.C. § § 235, 2330a, and 2463 and DOD guidance on the Inventory of Contracted Services.

DOD Has Ongoing Efforts to Collect Contractor Manpower Data, but Data System Issues Have Not Been Resolved

Over the past year and a half, DOD has taken its first steps to implement a November 2011 plan to collect contractor manpower data from contractors. These steps included directing components to start collecting direct labor hours and associated costs from contractors and initiating efforts to develop and implement a department-wide data collection system based on the Army's CMRA to collect and store inventory data, including contractor manpower data. AT&L and P&R officials estimate that the new system will be available in fiscal year 2014, with DOD components reporting on most of their contracted services by fiscal year 2016. DOD, however, is still working on key decisions related to security, funding, and other technological issues and has not developed an implementation plan with specific time frames or milestones to help ensure DOD remains on track to develop its planned data collection system. For the fiscal year 2011 inventory, DOD components generally used the same compilation processes used in the previous year. As such, with the exception of the Army, which already collects contractor manpower data and other key information using its CMRA data collection system, the remaining components obtained most of their inventory information from FPDS-NG, a system that does not collect contractor FTE information and has other limitations, which limit its utility for purposes of compiling a complete and accurate inventory.

DOD Has Taken Initial Steps to Implement a Department-wide Data Collection System

DOD has taken steps to meet legislative requirements to develop a data collection system that provides management insight on contracted services and collects the required data points for each contracted service, including information on the number of contractor FTEs. In April 2011, Congress passed the Department of Defense and Full-Year Continuing Appropriations Act, 2011, which among other things, required the secretaries of the military departments and the directors of the defense agencies, in coordination with P&R, to submit plans for documenting the number of contractor FTEs.[15] In response, in November 2011 DOD issued a plan to collect contractor manpower data and document contractor FTEs, and provided for short-term and long-term actions intended to meet the requirements of 10 U.S.C. § 2330a. DOD stated that it was committed to assisting components as they implement their plans, especially those currently without reporting processes or infrastructure in place, by leveraging the Army's CMRA system, processes, best practices, and tools to the maximum extent possible. Part of the long-term plan is to develop a comprehensive instruction for components to use on the development, review, and use of the inventories and for the Office of the Deputy Chief Management Officer, P&R, and other stakeholders to form a working group to develop and implement a common data system to collect and house the information required for the inventory, including contractor manpower data. DOD noted in its plan that it expects the data system to be operational and DOD components to be reporting on most of their service contracts by fiscal year 2016.

Over the past year and a half, DOD took a number of actions to implement its November 2011 plan.

---

[15]Pub. L. No. 112-10, § 8108(c).

- DOD published a Federal Register notice as required by the Paperwork Reduction Act,[16] in February 2012, seeking public comment on its proposal to allow DOD components to collect certain key information directly from contractors, including the number of direct labor hours associated with the provision of each service. The Office of Management and Budget approved DOD's request in May 2012.[17]

- In November 2012, the Under Secretaries for P&R and AT&L issued a joint memorandum that instructed components to ensure all actions to procure contracted services, including contracts for goods with defined requirements for services, include a requirement for the contractor to report all contractor labor hours required for performance of the services provided. The joint memorandum further instructed that data will be reported using an Enterprise-wide Contractor Manpower Reporting Application (eCMRA) and provided that the eCMRA website would be available to receive data to support the fiscal year 2013 inventory. Additionally, standard language, which was developed in a collaborative effort between AT&L, P&R, and the DOD components, is to be included in new statements of work and modifications to existing contracts.

  According to AT&L and P&R officials, DOD expects more than 270,000 contracts or orders to be modified across the department, with most contracts containing the language by fiscal year 2016. The Navy and Air Force began implementing the requirement to collect direct labor hours from contractors by modifying or including the reporting requirement in all their current and future service contracts in October and November 2012, respectively. The Army has previously included this requirement in its contracts.

- AT&L officials have also been working to develop a new provision to implement the reporting requirements in the Defense Federal Acquisition Regulation Supplement. As part of their efforts, they have

---

[16]44 U.S.C. §§ 3501-3521. The Paperwork Reduction Act requires that agencies obtain Office of Management and Budget approval before requesting most types of information from the public.

[17]The Army, which previously received approval from the Office of Management and Budget to collect certain contract data from contractors using its CMRA system, received a 3-year extension of this approval on December 15, 2011.

initiated a case to the Defense Acquisition Regulation Council, but as of April 2013, the case is still pending.

Further, the Navy and Air Force have each taken steps to develop their own interim system to collect and store contractor manpower data based on the Army's CMRA system. According to P&R and AT&L officials, the remaining DOD components will all share an interim CMRA-based system to collect and store their contracted services data. The Army and the Air Force will provide support for this component shared system; however, individual components will retain responsibility for ensuring the accuracy of the contracted services information reported into the CMRA system, which will later be used to compile the inventories.

In January 2013, P&R, in collaboration with DOD's Deputy Chief Management Officer, initiated efforts to develop and implement the department-wide eCMRA system that will replace the interim CMRA systems to collect and store information about all contracted services, including contractor reported labor hours and associated costs. The working group, comprised of officials from the Deputy Chief Management Office—whose role is to act as facilitator for the implementation of the system—and representatives from the military departments, has met several times as of April 2013 to discuss features of the new system.

P&R and AT&L officials stated that the department remains on track to meet the time frames outlined in DOD's November 2011 plan and indicated that they anticipate having the data collection system operational by fiscal year 2014. According to working group officials, however, the working group is still working on key decisions related to security, funding, and other technological issues and has not developed an implementation plan with specific time frames or milestones to help ensure DOD remains on track to meet its goals. Based on our discussions with several working group members, there is an unresolved issue about whether DOD components should use one department-wide system as planned or continue using the individual interim CMRA systems that have been developed. Some working group officials stated that using the multiple CMRA systems currently available was sufficient and would allow DOD to report accurate inventory data sooner. Conversely, other working group officials stated that a department-wide system would be less expensive to operate and upgrade and would be less of a burden on contractors because they would only have to interface with one DOD system. Working group officials did not provide any time frames for which a resolution to the issue would be made. Doing so in a timely fashion, as well as developing a plan of action with anticipated time frames and necessary resources, as we have previously recommended, would help facilitate the department's stated intent of collecting contractor manpower data.

DOD's Inventory of Contracted Services Continues to Be Based Primarily on FPDS-NG

In December 2011, AT&L and P&R issued guidance for the submission of the fiscal year 2011 inventory of contracted services. The guidance instructed the military departments and DOD components to use all reporting tools at their disposal to compile their inventories. In addition, it noted that the Director, Defense Procurement and Acquisition Policy would provide each component that has acquisition authority with a data set from the FPDS-NG that should be used to cross check the information that the components had compiled. The December 2011 guidance noted that most components were not currently collecting direct labor hours from contractors; therefore it identified five methodologies components could use singularly or in combination to estimate or calculate the number of contractor FTEs in their inventories. For example, components could collect direct labor hour information from contractors, or calculate the number of contractor FTEs by using a formula provided by P&R, which was based in part from information extrapolated from the manpower data collected by the Army from its contractors.[18]

Thirty-one DOD components submitted inventories for fiscal year 2011,[19] collectively reporting an estimated 710,000 contractor FTEs providing services to DOD with obligations totaling about $145 billion (see table 1).[20]

---

[18]DOD's December 2011 guidance also indicated that components could collect direct labor hours as reported by the contracting officer's representative for the service during fiscal year 2011; reference the independent government estimate or contractor technical proposals to extrapolate hours for the services provided in fiscal year 2011; or report information collected from contract invoices.

[19]A component's inventory submission may encompass contracts awarded on behalf of another component. For example, contracts for the Defense Acquisition University are reported by the Office of the Director, Administration and Management.

[20]According to AT&L and P&R officials, the difference in service contract obligations reported in the fiscal year 2011 inventory of contracted services, $145 billion, to the service contract obligations reported in FPDS-NG for fiscal year 2011, $199 billion, may be, in part, because the FPDS-NG obligation amount for services captures categories of services that are not reported in the inventory, to include lease or rental of equipment and facilities and military construction. In addition costs associated with utilities in the Utilities and Housekeeping product and service code, and freight and shipping in the Transportation, Travel and Relocation product and service code are also excluded.

Table 1: Summary of Contractor FTEs and Total Obligations As Reported in the Fiscal Year 2011 Inventory of Contracted Services

Component	Contractor FTEs	Total obligations
Army	246,916	$40,345,114,626
Air Force	166,496	$33,553,494,773
Navy	175,929	$32,728,959,199
Other components	120,538	$37,878,905,195
Total	**709,879**	**$144,506,473,793**

Source: GAO analysis of DOD data.

In comparison, for fiscal year 2010, DOD reported that 23 components submitted inventories, and estimated that about 623,000 contractor FTEs provided services with obligations totaling about $121 billion. DOD officials cautioned against comparing the number of contractor FTEs for fiscal year 2010 and fiscal year 2011 because components used different methodologies to estimate contractor FTEs, there were changes in the types of services that were to be included in the inventories, and other factors. For example, for the fiscal year 2010 inventory, DOD estimated contractor FTEs using one methodology for all components, other than the Army, while for the fiscal year 2011 inventory, those components used a variety of methodologies to estimate contractor FTEs.

Of the 31 components that submitted a fiscal year 2011 inventory of contracted services, only 2 components reported that they collected direct labor hour information from contractors—the Army, which uses CMRA, and the Defense Test Resource Management Center. Of the remaining components, 18—including the Air Force and Navy, which together represent almost half of the contractor FTEs in the inventory—reported that they used information extrapolated from Army manpower data and FPDS-NG to calculate an estimate of the number of contractor FTEs; 6 components reported that they used a variety of methodologies, including information from independent government estimates and contractor technical proposals; and 5 components did not identify the methodology used to estimate the number of contractor FTEs.

As we have previously reported, the FPDS-NG system has several limitations that limit its utility for purposes of compiling a complete and accurate inventory, including

- not being able to identify and record more than one type of service purchased for each contracting action entered into the system,

- not being able to capture any services performed under contracts that are predominantly for supplies,
- not being able to identify the requiring activity specifically,[21] and
- not being able to determine the number of contractor FTEs used to perform each service. [22]

Over the years, DOD has made a number of changes to address some of the limitations posed by using FPDS-NG, but not all of the limitations have been totally addressed. According to AT&L and P&R officials, the Army's CMRA system, as well as the CMRA-based systems now being used by the Air Force and Navy, will help the military departments overcome a number of the FPDS-NG limitations.

In addition to the limitations posed by using FPDS-NG as a source for compiling the fiscal year 2011 inventories, DOD experienced challenges with correctly identifying all services that were to be reported in the inventory. According to P&R and AT&L officials, the Air Force identified omissions of about $8 billion during its final review, for which the Air Force conducted a cross-check of its inventory data by comparing the FPDS-NG data set provided by Director, Defense Procurement and Acquisition Policy to its financial management system. AT&L and P&R officials noted that the omissions were primarily for services provided to the Air Force pursuant to a contract action conducted by other DOD components, and services provided to other DOD components pursuant to contract actions conducted by the Air Force. AT&L and P&R officials explained that they decided to report the omissions as "other DOD inputs" to avoid any further delays in submitting DOD's fiscal year 2011 inventory to Congress. According to Navy officials, the Navy did not identify errors, but noted that they did not use other systems to cross-check their inventory data. Army officials told us that the Army reported contracted services for which the Army was the requiring organization, but stated that other components may not have reported contracted services performed on their behalf pursuant to contract actions for which the Army was the procuring agency.

---

[21]The requiring activity is the organization charged with fulfilling a mission for or on behalf of DOD, and is responsible for delivering the service to satisfy the mission, even if the effort is contracted to the private sector.

[22]GAO-12-357.

Most Components Certified That They Conducted an Inventory Review, but Provided Limited Information to Gauge Review Efforts

Consistent with DOD's December 2011 guidance on the inventory review, most components certified that they conducted the inventory review, but provided only limited information of their review methodologies, results of their review, or use of the inventory to inform annual program reviews and budget processes. As of April 2013, 29 of the 31 components certified that they had completed a review of their inventory. AT&L and P&R officials stated that the requirement to submit certification letters represented a significant improvement over prior years' reviews when DOD could not determine whether or not the required reviews were conducted and believed that the letters provided useful insights into the components' processes and methodologies for conducting the reviews. Our analysis indicates, however, that none of the components reported on all six elements required in the guidance. For example, about half of the component letters provided limited or no information on the methodology used to perform the reviews. In addition, components provided limited information on their efforts to ensure appropriate government control when contractors were performing closely associated with inherently governmental functions. Further, while the Army and Air Force identified instances where contractors were performing inherently governmental functions and unauthorized personal services, they did not report whether they fully resolved these issues.

DOD's Fiscal Year 2011 Guidance Improved Accountability for the Inventory Reviews

In December 2011, AT&L and P&R issued guidance to components directing them to review at least 50 percent of their inventories and to the maximum extent possible, give priority to contracts not previously reviewed or those that may present a higher risk of inappropriate performance. In addition, heads of components were required to provide a letter to P&R by November 25, 2012, certifying completion of the inventory review and at a minimum include a discussion on the following six elements:

- an explanation of the methodology used to conduct the reviews and criteria for selection of contracts to review;
- delineation of the results in accordance with all applicable title 10 provisions and the December 2011 guidance;
- the identification of any inherently governmental functions or unauthorized personal services contracts, with a plan of action to either divest or realign such functions to government performance;
- the identification of contracts under which closely associated with inherently governmental functions are being performed and an explanation of steps taken to ensure appropriate government control

and oversight of such functions, or if necessary, a plan to either divest or realign such functions to government performance;

- the identification of contracted services that are exempt from private sector performance in accordance with DOD Instruction 1100.22, which establishes policies and procedures for determining the appropriate manpower mix; require special consideration under 10 U.S.C. § 2463; or are being considered for cost reasons, to be realigned to government performance;[23] and

- the actions being taken or considered with regards to annual program reviews and budget processes to ensure appropriate reallocation of resources based on the reviews conducted.

According to AT&L and P&R officials, the letters were intended to ensure that the components conducted the required review of their inventories, and documented the extent to which contractors were found to be performing certain functions to include inherently governmental and closely associated with inherently governmental and, to the extent necessary, provided for a plan to realign performance of such functions to government performance. DOD could also modify the statement of work or the manner of its performance to ensure that the work performed is not inherently government or divest or discontinue the work. In cases where contractors are performing activities that are closely associated with inherently governmental functions, DOD is required to ensure appropriate government control and oversight of such functions.

As of April 2013, 29 of the 31 components required to review their inventories had submitted a certification letter, while the Air Force submitted an interim letter based on a review of 30 percent of the contracts that it had completed at that time.[24] The Air Force provided us with updated figures based on their review of about 80 percent of their contract actions, which we incorporated in this report. However, the Air Force has yet to submit a formal letter to P&R certifying the results of its review. AT&L and P&R officials stated that the requirement to submit certification letters represented a significant improvement over prior

---

[23]DOD components may designate certain positions as commercial exempt for a variety of reasons, including esprit d' corps and professional development.

[24]The Defense Microelectronics Activity and US Forces Korea, which represent less than 1 percent of contract obligations in the fiscal year 2011 inventory, did not submit a certification letter. In addition to the 31 components, the Defense Intelligence Agency provided a certification letter in support of its classified inventory.

years' reviews when DOD could not determine whether or not the required reviews were conducted and believed the letters provided useful insights into the components' processes and methodologies for conducting the reviews.

Components Provided Limited Information in Certification Letters

Our analysis of the 29 component certification letters found that none discussed all six elements required in guidance. Further, certification letters varied significantly in terms of the information and insights provided for the methodologies components used to review their inventories, the results of the reviews, and use of the inventory to inform annual program reviews and budget processes, as illustrated in the following examples.

- Methodology and Selection Criteria: Sixteen of the 29 components provided information on both the criteria and methodology used to conduct their reviews. These components represent about 38 percent of the total contractor FTEs submitted in the inventory. However, the level of detail provided in the certification letters varied. For example, the Army, which noted in its certification letter that it reviewed more than 50 percent of its contracted functions, provided a detailed explanation of its selection criteria and review methodology.

  In its inventory submission, the Army explained that it has a two-pronged approach to reviewing the activities in the inventory. First, it uses a pre-award process that includes detailed checklists to help assess whether the proposed contract includes services that are inherently governmental functions or inappropriate personal services, and to identify services that are closely associated with inherently governmental functions. For example, to identify work that is closely associated with inherently governmental functions, the checklists ask whether the contractor will be providing services related to budget preparation, feasibility studies, and acquisition planning, among others. Second, it uses a post-award review, the Panel for Documentation of Contractors, to review information provided by commands to make certain determinations such as whether a contractor's performance of closely associated with inherently governmental functions has evolved into the performance of inherently governmental functions. The panel also evaluates whether sufficient capacity exists to oversee the contracted workforce. This process allowed the Army to identify over 900 contractor FTEs performing inherently governmental functions and over 44,000 contractor FTEs performing closely associated with inherently governmental functions.

In contrast, the Department of Defense Education Activity indicated its review was conducted by comparing data from the inventory with information gathered through their contract writing system database. The component provided no additional information on its methodology.

Based on the reported methodologies, we could not determine whether several components took into consideration the way an activity is performed or administered as part of their inventory reviews, which was required by the December 2011 guidance. For example, U.S. Special Forces Command indicated in its certification letter that all the contracts in its inventory were reviewed before award by the Special Operations Command Requirements Evaluation Board. The command did not indicate whether reviews were conducted after contracts were awarded. While the Office of Federal Procurement Policy directs agencies to confirm before award that the services to be procured do not include inherently governmental work, it also directs agencies to review on an ongoing basis the functions performed by contractors to ensure that the work being performed is appropriate.[25] It was unclear based on our analysis of the certification letters, however, whether U.S. Special Forces Command, as well as several other components, took into consideration the way a contract is performed or administered as part of their inventory reviews.

- Inventory Review Results: All 29 components included a discussion of inherently governmental functions and unauthorized personal services in their letters. However, 4 of the 29 components did not discuss whether contractors were performing functions closely associated with inherently governmental functions, and 20 of the 29 components did not discuss contracted services that are exempt from private sector performance. Therefore, we could not determine if these components considered these types of activities when conducting their inventory reviews or whether no instances were found.

Two components—the Army and Air Force—identified contractors performing inherently government functions or unauthorized personal

---

[25]Office of Federal Procurement Policy Letter 11-01, *Performance of Inherently Governmental and Critical Functions* (Sept. 12, 2011).

services. The other 27 components indicated that they did not have contractors performing any of these activities. Table 2 summarizes the number of contractor FTEs the Army and Air Force identified.

Table 2: Number of Contractors Identified as Performing Inherently Governmental Functions and Unauthorized Personal Services in the Fiscal Year 2011 Review of the Inventory of Contracted Services

Component	Inherently governmental contractor FTEs	Unauthorized personal services contractor FTEs
Army	936	718
Air Force	473	85

Source: GAO analysis of DOD data.

The Army, in its certification letter, noted that it planned to use term or temporary employees and/or military special duty personnel while awaiting insourcing approval of functions at risk of inherently governmental performance or otherwise lacking statutory authority. In January 2013, however, the Secretary of the Army froze civilian hiring, terminated temporary employees and prohibited extensions of term appointment without a specific exception to mission critical activities. In subsequent discussions with Army officials, we found that the Army, as of April 2013, had not developed a plan to address all instances in which contractors were performing inherently governmental functions or providing unauthorized personal services. Similarly, in follow-up discussions with Air Force officials, they told us that they are still discussing resolution of the instances identified with their manpower and personnel communities, as well as the affected major commands.[26]

Twelve of the 29 components identified contractors performing closely associated with inherently government functions (see table 3), 13 components noted that they did not have contractors performing these functions, and 4 did not discuss this element in their certification letter. Since DOD's guidance did not specify how components were to report the number of instances identified, components discussed the instances they found in a variety of ways. For example, the Army and the Air Force were able to provide us with the number of contractor FTEs performing closely associated with inherently governmental functions, while the Navy identified the number of contracts and the Defense Logistics Agency identified the percent of contracts that included this type of activity. As a result, it is difficult to determine how many contractors are performing closely associated with inherently governmental functions. Further, our prior work has found that DOD contracts for significant amounts of professional, administrative and management support services, a significant portion of which were services that closely supported inherently governmental functions.[27] Based on our prior work, it is not clear that DOD components accurately identified the extent to which their contractors are performing such functions during their inventory reviews.

---

[26]In April 2012, we reported that the Army and the Air Force had identified contractors performing inherently governmental functions through their reviews of the fiscal year 2009 inventories. See GAO-12-357. We recommended that the Secretaries of the Army and the Air Force take the necessary corrective actions to resolve the issues. DOD concurred with these recommendations. As of May 2013, the Army had resolved one case regarding the use of security contractors in Kwajalein Atoll by transferring responsibilities to government personnel. Further, Army officials noted that for the four instances of contractors performing system coordinator duties, the Deputy Director for Intelligence Systems instructed the contractors supporting his office that they were not authorized to represent the Army, were not to attend any meetings also attended by a member of congress or congressional staff, nor were they to identify themselves as Department of the Army Systems Coordinators in any correspondence or communication. The Army, however, has not provided information on the remaining two instances we recommended that it resolve. Air Force officials told us that the two instances identified in our report had been resolved, but did not provide information on the steps taken to resolve them.

[27]GAO, *Defense Acquisitions: Further Actions Needed to Address Weaknesses in DOD's Management of Professional and Management Support Contracts*, GAO-10-39 (Washington, D.C.: Nov. 20, 2009).

Table 3: Components Identifying Instances of Contractors Performing Closely Associated with Inherently Government Functions

Component	Closely associated with inherently governmental functions [a]
Army	44,541 contractor FTEs
Air Force	1,398 contractor FTEs
Navy	The Navy did not identify the number of contractor FTEs, but noted they have 25 contracts that contained these functions.
Defense Advanced Research Projects Agency	The agency did not identify the number of contractor FTEs in current contracts, but noted they have contracts that contained these functions.
Defense Logistics Agency	The agency did not identify the number of contractor FTEs, but noted that 4.5 percent of their sample of more than 50 percent of contract actions contained these functions.
Defense Commissary Agency	The agency did not identify the number of contractor FTEs, but noted that they had contractors performing these functions.
Office of the Secretary of Defense Washington Headquarters Service Pentagon Force Protection Agency [b]	The components did not identify the number of contractor FTEs, but reported that 24 out of 950 contracts consolidated from the three components had contractors performing these functions.
Defense Threat Reduction Agency	The agency did not identify the number of contractor FTEs, but noted that several contracts contained these functions.
United States Northern Command/ North American Aerospace Defense Command [c]	The commands did not identify the number of contractor FTEs, but noted that "some requirements" contained these functions.
TRICARE Management Activity	The activity did not identify the number of contractor FTEs, but stated that some contracts contained these functions

Source: GAO analysis of DOD data.

[a]With the exception of the Army and the Air Force, components did not identify the number of contractor FTEs performing closely associated with inherently governmental functions.

[b]The Office of the Secretary of Defense, Director of Administration and Management submitted a consolidated review on behalf of the Office of Secretary of Defense, Washington Headquarters Service and the Pentagon Force Protection Agency, but did not specifically identify which component reported it had contractors performing closely associated with inherently governmental functions.

[c]United States Northern Command/North American Aerospace Command submitted one inventory of contracted services and one review certification letter.

The 12 components' certification letters varied in the level of detail provided regarding the form of government control and oversight of contractors performing closely associated with inherently governmental functions. For example, the Defense Logistics Agency noted that it limits contractors' exercise of discretion, assigns sufficient government employees to oversee the work, and identifies contractors and their products to ensure they are not being confused with those of government employees. In contrast, the Defense Advanced Research Projects Agency, stated that it awards and administers contracts in compliance with all applicable procedures, but did not provide further detail.

Finally, 9 of the 29 components discussed contracted services that are exempt from private sector performance. None of these components reported having services exempt from private sector performance.

- Annual program reviews and budget processes: Fifteen of the 29 components that submitted review certification letters reported that they had used the information from their inventory reviews for annual program reviews or budget processes. For example, the Defense Contract Management Agency noted that it uses a review board to analyze service contracts on a monthly basis to look at requirements, follow-on contracts, and exercise of contract options proposed in the near future. In addition, it is currently assigning priorities and targeting reduction and conversions from contractors to government positions. These changes in priorities or workforce realignment would entail a change where funds are requested in budget justification materials. In another example, the U.S. Special Operations Command noted that it uses a requirements approval system to evaluate requirements, eliminate redundancies, and identify activities to be insourced. In addition, the Army has indicated that their inventory and inventory review were used to inform total workforce management reviews, including planned efforts to implement spending reductions for services that are closely associated with inherently governmental functions, and its fiscal year 2014 budget submission. None of the components, however, provided details on specific budgetary actions they took.

The Fiscal Year 2012 Inventory Review Guidance Requires Components to Provide Additional Information

DOD issued revised guidance applicable to the components' fiscal year 2012 inventories in February 2013. DOD components are expected to review 80 percent of their inventories and respond to the same six elements as they were required to do in fiscal year 2011, but the components will also be required to provide additional information on the funds and the number of contractor FTEs associated with the following functions:

- inherently governmental functions,
- closely associated with inherently governmental functions,
- critical functions,
- unauthorized personal services lacking statutory authority,
- authorized personal services, and
- commercial functions.

In addition, components are to provide an explanation of the degree to which the functions are part of overseas contingency operations, or reimbursable functions not currently in the component's budget estimate for contracted services. Further, components are to report on the actions taken with respect to the functions described above, including whether the contract where these functions reside is continuing or modified, or whether the function was insourced or divested.[28]

Conclusions

Since fiscal year 2002, Congress has directed DOD to increase visibility into the purchase of services by the department, in part through the establishment of a data collection system that would allow it to identify each activity being performed by contractors and make informed workforce mix and budgetary decisions. With the exception of the Army, DOD's overall progress to date can be characterized as a series of incremental, ad hoc steps, often taken in response to congressional direction. Over the past 18 months, DOD has been able to reach internal agreement on a way forward to collect contractor manpower data directly from contractors and has taken certain tangible steps toward this goal, such as by requiring components to begin modifying more than 270,000 contracts and task orders and to require new contracts to include provisions to require contractors to report direct labor hours, the types of functions being performed, and other information into interim CMRA systems. Nevertheless, it will be at least another year before DOD may have a department-wide eCMRA system in place to collect inventory data, such as manpower data directly from contractors and 2 more years, at the earliest, until it may have all components in compliance with inventory reporting requirements. Further, there are a number of challenges and unresolved issues that require continued management attention. For example, while DOD indicates that it remains on track to

---

[28]DOD defines insourcing as the conversion of any currently contracted service or function to DOD civilian or military performance, or a combination thereof. (Deputy Secretary of Defense, Insourcing Contracted Services—Implementation Guidance, May 28, 2009). To divest a service or function means to eliminate the service or function.

have a departmentwide data collection system in place in fiscal year 2014, the working group DOD established in January 2013 is still working on key decisions related to security, funding, and other technological issues and has not developed an implementation plan with anticipated time frames and necessary resources to help ensure DOD remains on track to meet its goals, as we recommended in 2011.

Similarly, DOD's December 2011 guidance has helped ensure that most components are reviewing their inventories. DOD also believes that the certifications by components have provided it better insights into the processes used and results of the reviews. Our review, however, indicates that the certifications often did not address or provided only limited information on the six elements that were called for by DOD's December 2011 guidance. Most significantly, the letters were inconsistent in describing the methodology used to identify and review the inventories, the actions taken or planned to be taken by the military services to address instances in which contractors were found to be performing inherently governmental functions or unauthorized personal services, or how these and other components were providing adequate government oversight of contractors who were performing work closely associated with inherently governmental functions. For example, the Army and Air Force identified instances where contractors were performing inherently governmental functions and unauthorized personal services, but did not report whether they fully resolved these issues. Further, based on our review of the certification letters, it is unclear the extent to which the differences in the approaches used to conduct the reviews contributed to the wide variation of instances identified with regard to contractors performing work that is closely associated with inherently governmental functions. For example, the Army identified over 44,000 contractor FTEs performing work closely associated with inherently government functions, while 13 components did not identify any instances where contractors were performing these functions.

Having the ability to identify and report instances of contractors performing inherently governmental functions, unauthorized personal services, or those closely associated with inherently governmental functions is one of the key benefits that the inventory is to provide to DOD, as it allows DOD to ensure contractors are performing appropriate work and to decide on the appropriate course of action should the reviews find that not to be the case. However, that value is significantly reduced if decision-makers have no assurance on whether corrective action was taken. DOD's February 2013 guidance that governs the fiscal year 2012 inventory review attempts to improve accountability of the funds allocated to certain high risk functions and obtain better insight into the resolution of instances where contractors are performing inherently governmental functions or unauthorized personal services. The results, however, hinge on the extent to which the components comply with the guidance. Based on this year's results, whether the components do so is not a foregone conclusion.

Recommendations for Executive Action

To ensure that the inventory of contracted services reviews provide greater context and value to DOD leadership, we recommend that the Secretary of Defense direct component heads to take the following two actions:

- Comply with DOD's February 2013 guidance, by ensuring that all required inventory review data elements, including a comprehensive description of their inventory review methodology, are addressed in their certification letters; and
- Provide updated information in certification letters on how they resolved the instances of contractors performing inherently governmental functions or unauthorized personal services in prior inventory reviews.

Agency Comments and Our Evaluation

DOD provided us with written comments on a draft of this report. DOD agreed with one recommendation and partially concurred with one recommendation. DOD's written response is reprinted in appendix II. DOD also provided technical comments, which were incorporated as appropriate.

DOD concurred with our recommendation that to provide greater context and value to DOD leadership, DOD should direct component heads to comply with its February 2013 guidance and ensure that all required inventory review data elements, including a comprehensive description of their inventory review methodology, are addressed in their certification letters. DOD did not believe that it was necessary for the Secretary of Defense to provide additional guidance, but rather indicated that AT&L and P&R, which have lead responsibility for the inventory, will disseminate our report to the components with a reminder that each component must specifically address each item listed in the fiscal year 2012 inventory of contracted services guidance. While we appreciate DOD's actions to address the recommendation, the fact that none of the components fully addressed each element contained in AT&L and P&R's

previous guidance underscores, in our view, the need for more direct involvement by the Secretary to ensure compliance.

DOD partially concurred with our recommendation that component heads provide updated information in certification letters on how they resolved the instances of contractors performing inherently governmental functions or unauthorized personal services in prior inventory reviews. DOD stated that while it agreed with the intent to ensure complete information is provided in certification letters regarding how component heads resolved instances of contractors performing inherently governmental or unauthorized personal services, DOD believes that the focus should be on the current and future reviews of the inventory of contracted services, rather than a correction of prior inventory reviews. To do so, DOD stated that AT&L and P&R will ask each component to include in the fiscal year 2012 certification letters any updated information on how they resolved the instances of contractors performing inherently governmental functions or unauthorized personal services in prior inventory reviews. DOD added that the fiscal year 2013 inventory of contracted services guidance will be updated to include this requirement when it is published in February 2014. Subsequently, DOD stated that any instances of contractors performing inherently governmental functions or unauthorized personal services recorded in prior inventory reviews that persist will be included and documented in the fiscal year 2012 and future review processes. DOD said it will verify that the certification letters contain a complete and accurate description of all required data elements, including actions taken to resolve outstanding issues related to contractors performing inherently governmental functions and unauthorized personal services prior to closing the respective review process. We agree that such an approach, if successfully implemented, would meet the intent of our recommendation.

We are sending copies of this report to the Secretary of Defense and interested congressional committees. In addition, the report is available at no charge on the GAO website at http://www.gao.gov.

If you or your staff have any questions about this report, please contact me at (202) 512-4841 or dinapolit@gao.gov. Contact points for our Offices of Congressional Relations and Public Affairs may be found on the last page of this report. GAO staff who made contributions to this report are listed in appendix III.

Timothy J. DiNapoli
Director, Acquisition and Sourcing Management

Appendix I: Objectives, Scope and Methodology

Section 803(c) of the National Defense Authorization Act for Fiscal Year 2010 directs GAO to report for 3 years on the inventory of activities performed pursuant to contracts for services that are to be submitted by the Secretary of Defense for fiscal years 2009, 2010, and 2011, respectively. To satisfy the mandate for 2012, we assessed (1) the progress DOD has made in compiling the inventory of contracted services and the status of efforts to collect contractor manpower data, and (2) the extent to which the defense components complied with DOD's December 2011 guidance for reporting on the review of the fiscal year 2011 inventories.

In performing our work we obtained pertinent documents and interviewed cognizant officials from the Office of the Under Secretary of Defense for Acquisition, Technology and Logistics (AT&L); Office of the Under Secretary of Defense for Personnel and Readiness (P&R); the Office of the Under Secretary of Defense (Comptroller); Office of Defense Procurement and Acquisition Policy; Deputy Chief Management Officer; the departments of the Army, Navy, and Air Force; and two DOD components–the Defense Logistics Agency (DLA) and Defense Information Systems Agency (DISA).

To assess the progress DOD has made in compiling the inventory of contracted services and the status of efforts to collect contractor manpower data, we reviewed the December 2011 guidance issued by AT&L and P&R related to the inventory compilation processes. We analyzed 31 DOD components' fiscal year 2011 inventory submissions and all memorandums accompanying the inventory submissions, to determine the methodologies and processes used when compiling the fiscal year 2011 inventories and calculating or estimating the number of contractor full time equivalents (FTE). We focused on the Army, Navy, Air Force, DLA, and DISA because they had among the largest service contract obligations and contractor FTEs in the fiscal year 2011 inventory. We include DOD's estimate of overall obligations and contractor FTEs for fiscal year 2011 in this report. We did not independently assess the accuracy or reliability of the underlying data supporting the components' inventories of contracted services. However, our previous work identified data limitations with DOD components using data from the Federal Procurement Data System-Next Generation (FPDS-NG) as the basis for their inventories. We discuss these limitations in the report, as appropriate.

In addition, we assessed DOD's progress in developing a common data system to collect and house contractor manpower data for the entire department. We reviewed guidance issued by AT&L and P&R on modifying new and existing contracts to require reporting of contractor manpower data, and discussed the implementation by the Air Force, Navy, and DOD components of an interim data system. We also interviewed officials from AT&L, P&R, and the Office of the Deputy Chief Management Officer, and the military services to obtain the status of efforts in developing and implementing a department-wide data system to collect and house contractor manpower information.

To assess the extent to which DOD components followed DOD's guidance on the review of their fiscal year 2011 inventory, we analyzed 29 inventory certification letters submitted to P&R as of April 2013. We assessed the letters to determine if components reported on the six elements in DOD's guidance for the inventory review, including the selection criteria and methodologies used to conduct the inventory reviews, a listing of the results of their compliance with applicable Title 10 provisions, workforce issues identified, whether the workforce issues had been resolved, identification of contracted services that are exempt from private sector performance, and actions being taken or considered with regards to annual program reviews and budget processes. We also followed-up with appropriate Army and Air Force officials to determine how they resolved workforce issues identified in their fiscal year 2009 inventory reviews. We did not assess whether the reported data or guidance met legislative requirements for the inventory review. In addition, we also did not independently assess the reliability and accuracy of the review certification information.

We conducted this performance audit from October 2012 to May 2013 in accordance with generally accepted government auditing standards. Those standards require that we plan and perform the audit to obtain sufficient, appropriate evidence to provide a reasonable basis for our findings and conclusions based on our audit objectives. We believe that the evidence obtained provides a reasonable basis for our findings and conclusions based on our audit objectives.

Appendix II: Comments from the Department of Defense

OFFICE OF THE UNDER SECRETARY OF DEFENSE
3000 DEFENSE PENTAGON
WASHINGTON, DC 20301-3000

ACQUISITION,
TECHNOLOGY
AND LOGISTICS

MAY 2 0 2013

Mr. Timothy J. DiNapoli
Director, Acquisition and Sourcing Management
U.S. Government Accountability Office
441 G Street, N.W.
Washington, DC 20548

Dear Mr. DiNapoli:

This is the Department of Defense (DoD) response to the GAO Draft Report, GAO-13-491, "DEFENSE AQUISITIONS: Continued Management Attention Needed to Enhance Use and Review of DoD's Inventory of Contracted Services," dated May 6, 2013 (GAO Code 121102). Detailed comments on the report recommendations are enclosed.

Sincerely,

Richard Ginman
Director, Defense Procurement
and Acquisition Policy

Enclosure:
As stated

GAO Draft Report Dated May 6, 2013
GAO-13-491 (GAO CODE 121102)

"DEFENSE AQUISITIONS: Continued Management Attention Needed to Enhance Use
and Review of DoD's Inventory of Contracted Services"

DEPARTMENT OF DEFENSE COMMENTS
TO THE GAO RECOMMENDATIONS

RECOMMENDATION 1: To ensure that the inventory of contracted services reviews provide
greater context and value to DOD leadership, the GAO recommends that the Secretary of
Defense direct component heads to comply with DOD's February 2013 guidance, by ensuring
that all required inventory review data elements, including a comprehensive description of their
inventory review methodology, are addressed in their certification letters.

DoD RESPONSE: Concur with comment. DoD does not feel that additional guidance from the
Secretary is required at this time. OUSD(AT&L) and OUSD(P&R), as leads for the Department
on the Inventory of Contracts for Services (ICS), will disseminate the GAO report with a
reminder that each Component must specifically address each item listed in the FY12 ICS
Guidance issued February 4, 2013. With this reminder, we will ask each Component to include
in the FY12 certification letters any updated information on how they resolved the instances of
contractors performing inherently governmental functions or unauthorized personal services in
prior inventory reviews. The FY13 ICS guidance will be updated to include this requirement
when it is published February 2014.

RECOMMENDATION 2: To ensure that the inventory of contracted services reviews provide
greater context and value to DOD leadership, the GAO recommends that the Secretary of
Defense direct component heads to provide updated information in certification letters on how
they resolved the instances of contractors performing inherently governmental functions or
unauthorized personal services in prior inventory reviews.

DoD RESPONSE: Partial-Concur with comment. While the Department agrees with the
GAO's intent to ensure complete information is provided in certification letters regarding how
component heads resolved the instances of contractors performing inherently governmental
functions or unauthorized personal services, DoD recommends the focus be on the current FY12
ICS reporting requirement and future reviews of the ICS, rather than a correction of prior
inventory reviews. Any instances of contractors performing inherently governmental functions
or unauthorized personal services recorded in prior inventory reviews that persist, will be
included in the FY12 and future ICS's and fully documented in the associated review processes.
DoD will verify the certification letters contain a complete and accurate description of all
required data elements, including actions taken to resolve outstanding issues related to
contractors performing inherently governmental functions and unauthorized personal services
prior to closing the respective review process.

Appendix III: GAO Contact and Staff Acknowledgments

GAO contact	Timothy J. DiNapoli, (202) 512-4841 or dinapolit@gao.gov
Staff Acknowledgements	In addition to the contact named above, Cheryl Andrew, Margaret A. Best, Laura Greifner, Katheryn S. Hubbell, Julia Kennon, John Krump, LeAnna Parkey, Guisseli Reyes-Turnell, and Wendy P. Smythe made key contributions to this report.

Please Print on Recycled Paper.

www.ingramcontent.com/pod-product-compliance
Lightning Source LLC
Chambersburg PA
CBHW080636290526
45790CB00007B/3088